'Top of the Morning'
Book of Incredibly Short Stories

selected by
Brian Edwards

National Radio

TANDEM PRESS

First published in New Zealand in 1997 by
TANDEM PRESS
2 Rugby Road, Birkenhead, North Shore City,
New Zealand

Reprinted 1997 (twice), 1998

ISBN 1 877178 14 4

Design and production by Graeme Leather
Printed in New Zealand by Brebner Print

The New Zealand Teenage Cancer Patients' Society

CanTeen is a peer support network for teenagers with cancer or life-threatening blood disorders, and for their teenage brothers and sisters. CanTeen believes that no teenager facing a diagnosis of cancer should ever have to go through this alone, and that the best people to support teenagers in this uncertain situation are other teenagers who have been though similar experiences.

Supporting its members through recreational and educational programmes, CanTeen relies on the generosity of the community to continue its services and receives no government funding. If you would like further information or can help in some way, please contact your local branch or the National Office as follows:

CanTeen New Zealand, PO Box 152, AUCKLAND
Tel: 09-373 3670
Fax: 09-373 3673
email: canteen@childcancer.org.nz

INTRODUCTION

This is a pretty unusual book. Unusual because it was written by a couple of hundred authors. Short story writers to be precise. Very short story writers. Each had the task of putting together a complete and compelling narrative in only fifty words, and those whose sterling efforts appear in these pages are a mere fraction of the 'Top of the Morning' listeners who rose to what must have seemed a near-impossible challenge. So I'd like to congratulate everyone who took part in the Incredibly Short Story competition. You all did brilliantly!

Running competitions for 'Top of the Morning' listeners and turning them into books is becoming something of a habit. *The Top of the Morning Book of Incredibly Short Stories* follows in the footsteps of *Top of the Morning Limericks* and *The Top of the Morning Book of Excuses*, both runaway successes. Royalties from those books went to two particularly worthy causes: the Make-A-Wish Foundation and the Royal New Zealand Foundation for the Blind, respectively. We're sticking to that habit, too. Royalties from this book will go to CanTeen, the national peer support network for teenagers diagnosed with cancer or life-threatening blood disorders, and for their teenage brothers and sisters.

I'd like to thank Bob Ross of Tandem Press, publisher of all three books, for his unflagging enthusiasm and support; Paper Plus for their generosity; and National Radio without whom there would have been no programme — and no listeners to write the stories.

There will, no doubt, be another competition and another book next year. That's the trouble with habits. Hopefully it will be as much fun as this one, both for the writers and the readers.

End of story.

Brian Edwards

Winners plus short-listed entries of the Top of the Morning Incredibly Short Stories competition are:

Dvořák String Quartet. Dark slow. Respectful auditorium tunes into each sad memorable phrase. Second violinist. Hair styled. Tuxedo adorns sexual puissance. Fingers. Second row female. Hair styled. Wears wicked purple. Demurrs.

Allegro appassionato. Eyes engage. Question? Answer. Finale. Applause.

Amidst excitement eyes meet. Final massive grins. No tonal ambiguities here.

Suzanne Gee, Ponsonby

HERBIE'S HAUNT

Secretly, she always hated that watercolour, bringing memories of those dreaded family holidays. Guiltily, she hid it after Herbie's death, years ago. Yesterday, defiantly, out it went to the jumble sale. But now — "Look, Grandma! We bought you this picture! Mum says it's the bay where you always went camping!"

Joan Woodward, Cashmere

A Market-Led Recovery

Unable to find work in legitimate theatre, Roger squatted in a decommissioned hospital. Despite his entrepreneurial flair, he failed to profit from Murder Mystery Weekends or Masked Balls for randy youth. Then a private hospice moved in and Roger finally found success with Death of Your Dreams — user-pays euthanasia.

JOHN SMYTHE, KELBURN

Morning. Dark and cold.

Quickly downstairs I race — hurry, hurry. Fling on coat, grab bag, throw open door. Cats scatter as I tear down the path. Can I do it?

Brakes squeal, heavy footsteps approach. My bag is whisked away and . . .

Yes, I almost missed the rubbish collection this week.

KAY FRANCIS, THORNDON

"**Y**ou've done it!" the scientist's assistant cried.

The pain and weariness of years of unremitting research fell from the old scientist's face.

"Yes," he agreed. "This is the cure . . . for everything."

He tested. Retested. It really worked.

Triumphantly he took his discovery to his sponsoring pharmaceutical firm.

They fired him.

GARTH GILMOUR, MILFORD

He moaned deliriously at the sight of the coiled leather strap, and searing passion surged through his veins at the recollection.

"Oh, Mistress," he panted, "let's do it again today."

Mandy stirred on the bed and opened one eye, sleepily.

"Shut up, Rover," she muttered. "No walkies till after breakfast."

BETTY LIVINGSTON, PALMERSTON NORTH

"For the first trial we'll only revert one minute," Potter said.
Inside the time machine Barlow nodded.

Potter threw the switch. After one minute Barlow looked out of the time machine at Potter.

"For the first trial we'll only revert one minute," Potter said.
Inside the time machine Barlow nodded.

TONY GIRLING, PICTON

THE ASSIGNATION

Guiltily, they exchanged glances. Lips meeting in passionate encounter, they melted together. Was it right, they wondered, locked in passionate embrace? She moaned in guilty passion; exploded in pleasure; and cried out at the climax. Fag ended sex as they relaxed warily.

"Do you think the kids heard?" he asked.

KELLY DUNCAN, CHRISTCHURCH

NOTHING CHANGES

My sister and I hadn't spoken since 1994; before that, 1990.

"Not my fault," she'd say.

Nor mine.

We spoke today.

In a carpark I backed into a backing car. Cr . . . unch!

"You've hit my car!" I screeched out the window.

My sister screeched back, "You hit mine!"

JEAN PICOT, TUAKAU

As a girl, Louise had jumped from each white island of the crossing to the next, avoiding edges. "Step on a line, marry a porcupine," they had sung. She remembers this, sitting in her garden-chair, sipping orange juice, glancing across at her snoring husband; pulling long thin splinters from her palms.

FRITH WILLIAMS, PAEKAKARIKI

"**C**ome to bed," she said. "It's 3 am."

She could see him in the half-light, hunched over the keyboard.

"Mm — well — half a mo," he said. "Just a sec."

"S'pose," she thought, trudging wearily down the hall, "that's what I get for marrying someone I met on the Internet."

LINDA BURGESS, PALMERSTON NORTH

MUTANT VIRUS

Virologist Geoff Smith focused his weary eyes on the laboratory results. The specimens tested were from human bodies found on a high country sheep station. In Australia the mutant rabbit calicivirus had already taken many lives. So far, none here. He scanned the page. His shoulders slumped. It had begun!

DAVE RUTHERFORD, CHRISTCHURCH

RISING DAMP

They met while paddling on the beach at Brighton. He took her boating at the Henley Regatta and courted her with romantic punt rides on the Thames. They celebrated their engagement with a barge holiday through the picturesque Essex Downs and then, after their wedding, a brief honeymoon aboard the *Titanic*.

RON MCINTOSH, WHANGAREI

Anton faced the starter's light on the Olympic ski jump.

He was confident of Gold in his new drag-free silk suit.

As he sped down the ramp, a loose thread caught in the timing cable.

His pants unravelled.

Slowing, in mid-air, he wished he was born a girl.

BARRY BAIN, ARROWTOWN

THE VOUCHER

"It's your choice. I'd advise flowers."

The girl fingered her voucher.

"Mmm, I love violets."

"Roses? Lilies?" suggested the assistant.

The girl frowned. "Too funereal."

The assistant smiled.

The girl's quandary deepened. Which? Choose!

Clustered butterflies? Daisies? No.

"Ahh, that's it. I'll have the bee!"

The tattooist accepted her voucher.

LORRAINE BLAIN, NELSON

It was love at first sight.

"Marry me," he said, "and I will take you to the ends of the earth."

She was a good judge of character, so she did.

They went to live in Invercargill and lived happily ever after.

He kept his word.

She knew he would.

MAUREEN GRAHAM, NORTH BEACH

LOVE AMONG THE COWSLIPS

Sir Walter Raleigh looked over the wall to where Queen Bess was sunning herself.

He felt the stirring in his loins which she always awoke in him.

Unable to contain his ardour, he leapt the wall and was on her.

"Best bull we ever had," Dave proudly told his wife.

DOROTHY BATES, FEATHERSTON

It was kind of scary, trying to sleep in the dark, empty house, miles from anywhere.

Damn the removal company for being a day late — and the power board too!

She thought she heard something and, groping for the matches to strike a light, felt them put into her hand.

JEAN GREGSON, CHRISTCHURCH

A New Beginning

She plunged the knife in. Satisfaction overwhelmed her as she felt the blade cut through the flesh.

The pressure had been building up all afternoon and now at last she felt vindicated.

No more excuses. No more guilt. No more self-loathing.

Her days on the vegetarian diet were over.

BEV THORNTON, HAMILTON

16

At a glance I could see he was special! Our eyes met. I knew this was it.

I felt drawn — like a magnet he compelled me to surrender. I was his captive. I moved closer, wound down the window, trembling with anticipation, I took his note.

It read — Transport Dept. Speeding Ticket Fine $50.

Ruby Sanders, Papakura

Catastrophe

Morgan hated cats. He took pot shots at them with an airgun, nailed up neighbours' cat flaps, kept a Dobermann in the garden, and put liver salts in their milk. Coming home from the pub, he tripped over a tabby, fell under a bus, was killed and reincarnated as a mouse.

Steve Matthews, Swanson

"You're 38 and not married. Are you a homosexual?"

"No Dad — you married at 25; were you a homosexual till then?"

"Of course not — oh, here is your stepmother."

"Hello, darling!"

"I was just talking to my son."

"I was addressing your son as darling — we are running away together."

BILL HUMPHREY, KOHIMARAMA

CHANGE

The long and soporific meal ended in drowsiness. He clad himself for sleep and fell into oblivion. Dreams of floating on air engendered his metamorphic juices. Awakening and casting off the mantle of sleep, he felt the twin desires for food and sex. The butterfly took its first flight.

SANDY WINTERTON, MELROSE

"The plan is foolproof," they'd said. So why was he in this appalling situation? Damn them! He should have hired a professional, taken out a "contract". Swallowing the bile burning his throat, he frantically read again his instructions. The words mocked him: "This kitset can be assembled in twenty minutes."

BILL DENGEL, OAKLANDS

Kathy sat thinking. Wally had always done the thinking. For forty years Wally had thought for both of them. Wally was smart, Wally knew everything — but now Wally lay dead. Kathy thought hard. "What shall I say to the police when they come and where shall I hide the gun?"

MARGARET FARR, WELLSFORD

"Yeah, mate. Built this fence meself. Nuthin' to it. Whack the old plumb line down, dig the holes, bit a concrete, few four b' two's 'n planking. Bang 'em up and she's done. Who needs a builder? Double the cost, eh?"

"Indeed," replied the stranger, a building inspector by trade.

ISLAY McLEOD, BROOKLYN

BLIND JUSTICE

"You are a thorough-going scoundrel," the judge told the shearer. "Your shameless tax evasion has robbed this nation of vital revenue. Society cannot tolerate such despicable behaviour. You will go to prison for twelve months."

Not a bad day's work, thought the judge. Now, where is my expenses claim form?

GRAHAME GILLESPIE, KELBURN

BEATING THE ODDS

He knew about statistics. She, uneducated, needed guidance.

"Don't gamble like your stupid family," he counselled. "They'll always be poor."

When her sister won Lotto he could barely disguise his rage.

"But darling," she smiled obediently, "*you* said I mustn't spend more than five dollars for her birthday present."

GAYLE BRUCE, AVONHEAD

Brenda's hand was frozen and trembling. "My God, what now?" she thought as the body lay rigid before her. Brenda and the walls were covered with blood. She dropped the knife from her hand, screaming, "Why . . . why . . . why can't they make giblet bags easier to get out of frozen chickens?"

RACHEL WIGHTMAN, MILTON

THE NEW IMMIGRANTS

1974 Auckland International Airport — arrival — excitement. Sparrows in the canteen — quaint. New Plymouth — black sand — Mt Taranaki — beautiful — is it dormant? Bring a plate — empty! Barefooted to school — wow! Jandals or flipflops? Sandflies (no one told them). Earthquake! Nothing familiar — no memories here. "She'll be right" — will they? Oh, England.

SHEILA WATERS, BLENHEIM

Braveheart the knight smashed through the castle gates and raced to the tower where his queen was held captive. He fought past the guards and up to the top room. The door was barred, but Braveheart kicked it down. It fell on his queen and killed her. "Oops," said Braveheart.

DAVID EMSLIE, ANDERSONS BAY

Who is the Boss?

He's passed out, from drinking. When he wakes he'll start again, yelling, throwing things and being physical.

I am stronger, smarter and more articulate than him, but he still dominates me completely. I must obey him or wear the consequences. Maybe, when he's one, he'll be nicer to his mother.

JAYE O'CONNOR, GERALDINE

Doggone!

Tried that new perfume today with pheremones to attract the opposite sex.

Some result! Came from miles around, fought over me — dogs, that is. Thought me a bitch on heat. Climbed tree to escape. Someone called fire brigade. So embarrassing!

But guess what? Got a date with a hunky fireman.

IRIS MELVILLE, DARGAVILLE

He came in sneezing.

"I've got the flu," he whimpered.

"Go to bed," she said.

She tended him with hot lemon, aspirin and love. She offered sympathy and soothed his fevered brow.

After five days he was recovered.

She caught it and collapsed into bed.

He went to the pub.

SUSAN SIDDLES, TARADALE

Another Saturday morning in the stale and shabby studio. The ageing announcer chokes back corrosive bitterness at the unseen audience, too stupid to comprehend the value of his work. *Bastards!*

Pulling the microphone closer, mustering an enthusiasm he doesn't feel, he speaks: *"The train now standing at Platform Seven . . . "*

CHRIS MITSON, WELLINGTON

Eleanor hesitated. She'd had a bad week — a death in the family, dinner with Fred's boss. But excuses meant nothing to these bastards. She took a deep breath and stepped up.

"Well done Eleanor, half a kilo."

Dizzy with relief, she sat down. It was over. For another week, anyway . . .

AMANDA CLOW-HEWER, ONERAHI

COSMIC KARMA

While scientists focused on global warming, believing humanity's puny efforts relevant, the asteroid swooped ever closer. It struck Antarctica. The vast ice-shelf melted and half the planet's coastline drowned. Entire nations vanished. Survivors tilled new soil, painfully rebuilding old skills and rueing their lost libraries. Few recalled the Internet.

MARCO OVERDALE, SEATOUN

"The trouble with you," she shouted, "is that you never say a word."

"But . . . " he tried.

"What's wrong?" she screamed. "Are you tongue-tied?"

"I . . . " he stammered.

"Why did I ever marry you?" she continued.

"Sorry . . . "

"It's no use being sorry!" she yelled. "Now we're running out of time!"

"Goodbye."

ALAN BOLLARD, WELLINGTON

Major McAdam stood by the ship's rail. Dark-eyed Poupette in Paris was with him and part of him, and would be always. He scattered the torn picture of her into the dark waters below. A blonde wife with chiselled profile and cool eyes awaited him. The war was over.

MARY BENNETT, WAIKANAE

Anything You Can Do . . .

Elliot scrambled from the bridge parapet, tears of humiliation burning his eyes. He couldn't even kill himself!

"The bitch," he raged, "running off with that rich bastard Tony!"

He never saw the Volvo that smashed into him, tumbling him along the motorway.

The woman passenger screamed. "Tony! You've killed someone . . . "

Sue Underwood, St Heliers

Off the Shelf

Their eyes met, briefly, over the frozen chickens. He saw her later, in Produce, fingering the zucchinis. He squeezed an aubergine. She glanced away. After the checkout she approached him. He smiled. He'd heard of this happening. She spoke: "Supermarket security. Would you step aside please and empty your pockets?"

S Naylor, Island Bay

MAX

"I've left my husband," she confided.

Beady-eyed, hawk-nosed, she fluttered, predatory, around mine. "The Parrot", we called her privately, and laughed.

Yesterday, I couriered his cockatiel to their lovenest. Quite a talker, little Max. Twenty phrases, all unmistakably in my voice.

Another large-beaked bird for his collection.

SUZANNE MITCHELL, MAUNGARAKI

PHONEY

The traffic was piled up. There had been an accident. The woman ran along the line of cars. She saw a man talking into a cell phone and knocked on his window. He ignored her. She opened his door. "Call an ambulance!" The man reddened. His phone was a toy.

JEAN ADEANE, RAUMATI BEACH

LIFE AFTER BRIAN

The Last Man On Earth shuffled through the ruins of nuclear devastation, the silence of the land echoing the loneliness in his heart.

Suddenly, a cry to his left revealed a woman. Visions of a new Eden crashed into his mind.

"My name's Adam, what's yours?"

"Oh," she said, "Ethel . . . "

IAN MILNES, PAKURANGA

The long war years had tested her faith. She had lost much, and cried often. But finally her prayers were heard. She had survived, and would soon be blessed with a child. Knowing that peace would come from heaven above, she gave thanks for another bright August dawn in Hiroshima.

SIMON GARNER, PARNELL

Simon's plan had worked. Ingratiating himself with his boss, Henry, and then Henry's wife; engineering Henry's "accidental" death whilst hunting; then marrying Henry's wealthy widow who also died "accidentally" whilst swimming, leaving everything to Simon. Perfect!

A future of luxurious travel beckoned.

Simon laughed aloud as he boarded the *Titanic*.

JOHN EGAN, WOBURN

JUSTICE

I siphoned his fuel and caused other delays to make him late home. Then I wrote anonymously to his wife that he was having an affair. I planted panties in his briefcase and sent a Valentine to his home address. Now I'm even with Dad for making me eat broccoli.

SANDY WINTERTON, MELROSE

REVENGE

She'd charmed me all morning. Blonde, manicured, all smiles.

"You remember me, then?"

"To be honest — no."

"Rosedale College. 1978. You dumped me. Wanted to spread your wings. Life experience you called it."

My face fell. "Lynne Dobson?"

"About your application. We're wanting more technical scope. And more life experience."

SUE DOW, PALMERSTON NORTH

In Tangiers I met Rabat. At 3am in a Kasbah cafe, after visiting sleazy bars, Rabat said, "Will you take two kilos of opium to Gibraltar?" and departed to pee against a wall.

Suddenly he was arrested by two gendarmes.

It is a criminal offence to urinate in the Kasbah.

REG TURNER, PYES PA

"**M**urder?" private eye Farlow asked. "Tell me."

She shuddered. "He was lying on the floor. The look on his face. Awful."

"How was he killed?"

"Two bullets in the back."

Farlow called the police. "I've got a killer here."

The cops burst in. Found Farlow alone. Shot in the face.

GARTH GILMOUR, MILFORD

In solitary confinement time dragged relentlessly. Sounds of everyday life tortured him through the walls of the darkened room. The approaching clatter of breakfast inspired a desperate, almost unthinkable, escape plan. He braced himself for action.

"Mum," he said. "The spots are fading. Please can I go back to school?"

KATHY MACDONALD, MT EDEN

John always craved fame. Recognition.

He excelled scholastically. Nobody noticed.

He played great soccer. Few cared.

He mastered the stock market, amassed a fortune. None commented.

In 1987, bankrupted, he slaughtered his entire family.

He led the news in all the media.

GARTH GILMOUR, MILFORD

AN OFF DAY

Fiftyish Grace Allsop, browsing through a store, found herself pitying a downtrodden-looking woman on a TV screen. Poor old soul, she thought, then realised she was actually only seeing a reflection of a passer-by. She glanced around. There wasn't another person in sight. She fled home.

MARIE CAMERON, BEACHLANDS

A New Day

He drifted into wakefulness, and remembered — school holidays had just begun.

Great!

He wondered what he, Smithy and Jake would do today. Swimming hole? Help Smithy's father with his horses?

He drifted back to sleep.

The nurse said, "He's gone — just three days short of the Queen's telegram."

DOROTHY BATES, FEATHERSTON

Night Visitor

I lay in bed very still, aware of the movement in the semi-darkness around me. I opened my eyes with the gentle click of the door closing. I felt the pillow case at the foot of my bed. I hadn't been asleep. I hadn't even been good all year!

LAURIE MURRAY, TOKOROA

The Interior Decorator

Three-day-old stubble parted into a tobacco-smelling yawn. His big toe protruded through his sock below the too-short crimplene trousers.

While picking a piece of stale beef from his teeth, he heard his wife farewelling the visitor.

"Who was that?" he grunted.

"The interior decorator. He says you'll have to go."

Carmel Hurdle, Bulls

Terror

He languished in jail, his frequent attempts to escape always unsuccessful. Feeling safe I strolled down Pall Mall, rented a house in Whitechapel Road and caught a train from Kings Cross. Then I heard he'd been released — a deadly threat once more. Who said Monopoly was a boring game?

Sybil Gregson, Wellington

For the Love of Penny

Penny was gorgeous, absolutely stunning. She had everything a guy could wish for. Lenny couldn't believe his luck. She had chosen him above everyone else. He possessed her: she was his very own love. She was sleek and sporty, and he loved that purring sound when he pressed her accelerator.

Ann-Kristen Leys, Remuera

Flint strikes steel when they are introduced. Meg and Oscar play it cool. Celebrities, every move observed. So, gently flirtatious, outcome not yet inevitable, but situation definitely promising: item in the making! Then Oscar, gobsmacked, renounces discretion, flagrantly displays his ardour. Meg's nostrils quiver. "Thank God," breathes the stud owner.

Norma Michael, Wellington

Everyone was waiting.

She looked tenderly into his eyes as she gently slipped on his ring.

"I am so sorry," she thought, "I know I will hurt you, but I have to do this."

Later, she watched him with his mother.

"You'll be fine," she murmured. She hated docking.

BETTY IRONS, PALMERSTON NORTH

LAST LAUGH

Cyril lay dying. Henry was going to miss his old friend's jokes and devilry.

"Closer," Cyril beckoned.

Henry moved cautiously towards him.

"Closer," Cyril gasped again. He feeble hand clutched Henry's arm.

Henry bent down to hear his last words.

Cyril was triumphant with his dying breath. "Tag you last!"

BARBARA NEWBURGH, CHRISTCHURCH

She felt panicky, the blackness engulfing her as arms reached out, tugging at her hair. Now around her neck, making her gasp. Her body swayed as she tried to free herself from the dark terror. Suddenly, a voice.

"I'm sorry madam, we only have that black dress in size 10."

N S WOODHOUSE, TRENTHAM

A FEISTY LADY

"The statue of Our Lady of San Paulo cries because she has an inbuilt refrigeration unit holding a tray of ice," he announced.

The statue broke into a loud belly laugh.

"Tape recording," he announced, agitated.

The crowd nodded, the Lady of San Paulo held two fingers high.

SIMON WILLIAMSON, LYALL BAY

LIFE: A NOVEL

Conception   "Yes, do it!"

Birth   "Aaaaahhhh!"

Rebellion   "Why can't I do it?"

Experimentation   "Why don't we do it?"

Marriage   "I do."

Parenthood   "Why did we do it?"

Adultery   "How could you do it?"

Playing the field   "How did I use to do it?"

Impotence   "Can't do it!"

Death   Done it.

ANNETTE WILLIAMS, CHRISTCHURCH

Sailing

The wind screamed in the rigging and the tattered sails cracked like pistol shots as the small yacht staggered over the towering swells and down the other side.

Continuously swept with stinging spray, the man and boy crouched in the cockpit.

"Are we having fun yet, Dad?"

"Yes!" he yelled.

ZOE BATTERSBY, PICTON

Big black Satan, Farmer Joe's best mouser, kept disappearing. Joe tracked him to Willow Farm, owned by a young widow.

"Could I buy Satan?" she asked. "Jamie doesn't talk since his father died, but he talks to that cat, they're inseparable."

"Take him," grunted Joe. "Worst mouser I ever had . . . "

AMANDA CLOW-HEWER, ONERAHI

Madeline cleared her throat, tried a few tentative hums and "La Las", then seated herself nervously with the other auditioning hopefuls. Not young, but always chorally dependable, she just yearned to join this highly rated choir.

"Next!"

Shaky start, but kind judges.

"Accepted. Music, wings and harp on next cloud."

JUNE DOWNIE, CHRISTCHURCH

THE PENTEKON BIBLE

God made, Adam bit, Noah arked, Abraham split. Joseph ruled, Jacob fooled, Bush talked, Moses balked; Pharaoh plagued, people walked. Sea divided, tablets guided, Promise landed. Saul freaked, David peeked, prophets warned, Jesus born. God walked, love talked, anger crucified, hope died. Love rose, Spirit flamed, Word spread, God remained.

REV DANA LIVESAY, WANGANUI

Mean Old Sam

Sam knew this was the end. As pain gripped his heart he frantically sliced his money into small pieces. Smiling through his agony, he pushed the last fragments through his blue lips.

"Who said you can't take it with you?" he gasped, drifting off into a state of joyous bliss.

B Cardno, Mt Victoria

The Last Say

The waiter entered the kitchen and placed his tray on the counter.

"Your last night, Chef, and the restaurant's booked out."

The chef walked to the kitchen door and peered through the glass porthole.

"Perfect," he muttered.

Moving over to the power box, he reached up and pulled the switch.

Nicki Waters, Napier

CONGRATULATIONS, LOUISE

The midwife laid the baby across her knees, then handed her the phone. Charles would marry her now. Louise dialled his office. He would be back from Singapore. Business took him away so much. Charles answered.

"Darling," she gasped, "you have a lovely son."

"How wonderful, but who is speaking?"

JOYCE POWELL, ONEHUNGA

THE BUNKER

The President sat alone in the bunker. It was all over. The last bombs had fallen. The last nightingale had sung in Central Park. There was nothing left. He was the last man alive on Earth. There was a knock at the door . . .

TERRY MORROW, TAUPO

A Friend in Need

Driving home, eyes moist with tears, Josephine realised what a fiasco the honeymoon had been. His drinking, his flirting, the endless arguments had left her sickened, heart broken and humiliated.

Caressing her softly, Antonio blew seductively into her ear and whispered, "Hush my darleeng, you are vell reed of heem."

Ron McIntosh, Whangarei

Catharsis

"Thank you for your letter of the 12th from which I formed the inevitable conclusion that you are a greedy and jealous pipsqueak. I have never read a wish-list of such self-centred claptrap from such an insignificant squirt."

"Well, now that's out of my system," said Father Christmas.

Sandy Winterton, Melrose

THE CURE

The doctor studied his patient with satisfaction. He was responding beyond expectation. Cases of inferiority, lack of confidence and paranoia were notoriously difficult to cure. The patient needed the doctor no longer, and as he took the gun out, pointed it and fired, realised that this was his final appointment.

JIM DIGGLE, HILLSBOROUGH

Approaching the crossing, Harriet sees a woman dressed exactly as she is. "Fancy that!" Even the bobbed hair is the same, one unruly cowlick protruding from the fringe. Then Harriet sees her husband. He links arms with the woman and they walk off together. Harriet's life passes before her eyes.

FRITH WILLIAMS, PAEKAKARIKI

ENVY

Ignore it! Don't call nurse! If Brenda dies, I can have her bed facing the window. She's been describing the family across the street; mother shopping, children playing, pretty daughter kissing boyfriend . . .

Brenda died last night. I'm being moved. At last! See for myself! No! A blank wall!

ESME PAGETT, NELSON

"Henry, you've locked the bathroom door again! Remember? The doctor says you shouldn't with your weak heart. Hurry with your bath. We leave for the Home at eleven and it's after ten. I've laid out clean clothes on top of your suitcase."

Henry waited, then snuggled lower, and smilingly drowned.

PATRICIA RAINEY, UPPER HUTT

Daylight

"**B**e brave," he muttered to himself.

The black tunnel loomed ahead, mysterious, damp, unending. With thumping heart he pushed on until a glimpse of light spurred him forward.

Then he was screaming as a blinding glare engulfed him, hands seized him roughly and a voice shouted, "It's a boy!"

FAYE LEAN, AVONSIDE

All at Sea!

The ship's captain had died after fifty years at sea. First Officer Simpson went to the skipper's deck with its one locked drawer. What was in there that the captain needed to inspect three times daily? The key turned easily and, opening the drawer, he read "Starboard — right, Port — left".

JIM DIGGLE, HILLSBOROUGH

DEAD LETTER

"I'll be the death of you," she vowed at their divorce.

But she died first.

After the funeral a letter arrived, addressed in her familiar hand.

Hate mail? Or second thoughts? It haunted him.

Years later he overdosed, the envelope in his grasp.

Unopened.

Inside, a blank sheet of paper.

HUNTLY ELIOTT, MT EDEN

I KILLED THE KING OF THE JEWS

After Pilate's verdict, the disciples fled and Jesus had to hump his own cross. When nailed up he started wailing about being forsaken; taking pity on him, I thrust my spear in under his ribs. I sometimes wonder whether he would have made anything of himself, if he had lived.

M CAMERON POLLOCK, SUSSEX, ENGLAND

DR FRANKENSTEIN

Lightning flashed. The monster sat up.

The scientist clasped her hands. "My God!" she said.

"Yes?" said the monster. "And you are . . . ?"

"Your creator," she announced, proudly.

"Nonsense!" Outraged. "You're a woman!"

"And so are you."

"What?" Even more outraged.

"Naturally, we always create in our own image."

ISA MOYNIHAN, CHRISTCHURCH

ON THE FACE OF IT

She was sitting on the fence. The sun warmed her as she gazed into the face of the young girl in the photograph. What had happened? Where had it gone? Her life! As she slowly put the picture down she knew that she had spent it, sitting on the fence.

NOELINE GAMBONI, HATAITAI

Remember!

Frail, elderly, at a corner table. It's her! Thirty years ago. They'd always met in cafes. She peers at him. He'd loved those blue eyes, now dimmed. Remembered secret meetings, shared joys. She stands, comes toward him. That same walk. She pauses near him.

"Stop . . . staring . . . at me!"

Walks on.

BRIAN TAYLOR, WAIKANAE

Almost

"Search warrant," he heard, as they pushed past him into the house.

"Why now?" he thought, heart pumping, pulse racing.

"Carol went missing three years ago, not the garden — please."

"Mr Craven," the intrusion startled him. "The key to your desk."

"Next door," he shrieked uncontrollably, "Craven lives next door."

ANDREW WICKHAM, WAIUKU

FIRST BEER

The journey from England over, the engineer and his wife settled into their Christchurch hotel. His wife retired. Time to sample his first kiwi brew.

He sensed the stares as the impressive container reached his lips. His eyes scanned the bar. The locals had small glasses alongside their jugs!

MIKE MARSHALL, CHRISTCHURCH

"You need glasses," she said.

"No, I don't," he said. "The type is smaller."

"It isn't. You're getting short-sighted."

"No, I'm not."

"They're doing free tests at the mall. Why don't you go?"

The first thing he said when he came home with his new glasses was, "You've got wrinkles."

FRANK NERNEY, HELENSVILLE

Mini Minimises her Adjectives

The writer met Mini Saga at a seminar. She wore a minimum of words and her meaning was clear, unlike his lady friend, Ms Story, who was adorned with adjectives. He soon became infatuated with Mini's form and style. So he abandoned Ms Story and embraced Mini — symbolically of course.

Bryce Hadfield, Mairangi Bay

They lay in bed; he, elderly, and she of younger years, contemplating their varied and ultimate futures.

"Will you remarry when I'm gone?"

"Oh yes," was her immediate reply.

"And will you gift my golf clubs to this intended beau?"

"Of course not, silly billy!" she responded.

"They're right-handed!"

D P Cox, Onetangi

Love Story

"**N**ever nibble nipples nicely, Nigel," nattered nubile Nora, "nibble naughtily."

Nodding nonchalantly, naïve Nigel nuzzled Nora's nifty nipples nebulously.

"No, Nigel," nagged Nora, "now nibble nastily!"

Nigel nervously navigated Nora's naked nipples, nibbling noncommittally.

"Nigel not need nooky?" needled neglected Nora.

"No," negatived Nigel, "Nigel never need nobody. Nigel narcissistic."

John Veal, Stokes Valley

The Homecoming

Fifteen years had elapsed, the door opened slowly.

"Hello, Granddad, remember me?"

"Ken lad, come in, sit down. I'll put the kettle on."

He heard the front door open again.

"Ken? How did you get in?" asked Auntie Kath.

"Granddad let me in."

"But, Ken, Granddad died five years ago!"

Dave Durnford, Christchurch

Birthday Toast

"Happy birthday to you," croaked the old woman, lifting her glass in a toast. The figure opposite gave no response. Berating her husband for an ingrate, she thumped her glass vigorously on the table. The desiccated skull opposite tumbled to the floor and the skeletal hand waved in macabre mockery.

J S Fisher, Christchurch

Arrival, cold, feeding, warmth, elimination, changing, powdering, adoration, faltering, growing, eating, progressing, changing, yearning, palpitating, grasping, conjugation, exquisite joy, fear, flight, growing, fancying, waiting, needing, building, mating, parenting, building, working, boredom, losing, yearning, escaping, sinning, exquisite joy, pain, remorse, settling, observing arrival, feeding, changing, powdering; stability, peace, feeding, cold, departure.

Bill Humphrey, Kohimarama

CONFESSION

Forgive me, Father, for I have committed the sins of lust (I think you are absolutely dishy); envy (of your charming housekeeper); pride (I think I am much sexier than she is); gluttony (I overcompensate by gorging on chocolates); and deceitfulness (for not reporting all this to my Mother Superior).

Grahame Gillespie, Kelburn

DRIFTING

Friday. Frank the drunk shot Rose, threw her overboard, and flaked out. Saturday. Hangover, no memory, wondering where she was.

"Frigging blackout again ... gotta dry out."

"Ditto, Frank."

Frank turned. "Rose! Been swimming? Kinda missed you."

Rose blew Frank's brains out.

"Yeah, you kinda did. Any towels on this tub?"

Bill Noble, Dunedin

SECOND CHANCE

Newly widowed, I knew what this stranger was going through. I wrote a note, baked him a cake. Later he returned the tin. "Come to a concert next week?" I ventured. "One condition — I take you to dinner first." He wooed me relentlessly — we married. Best cake I ever made!

Anne Wall, Waikanae

Harold couldn't believe she'd beaten him. Fifty word stories were hard work and to rub it in she'd written it on his cigarette paper while nagging him to quit. It lay in front of him — simply brilliant. Harold sulked. Then he slowly smiled as he reached for his tobacco tin.

CHRIS KNOPP, TE ANAU

INTERLUDE

The voice again — perfectly modulated, full of promise. Idly she wondered what he looked like, and if he had chosen the music. Irresistible music, that wooed her into submission and acceptance. Another voice, younger this time, lacking the peaches and cream of his predecessor.

"Telecom here. Can I help you?"

GRACE SWALES, KAITAIA

Decked out in golden yellow
A body slim and gently curved.
Elegant — desirable.
A vision to behold!
Stripping now — slowly,
The yellow mantle,
Peeled off piece by piece.
The soft creamy flesh exposed.
My desire mounting — barely contained!
At last to hold, to devour,
I bite into —
My beautiful banana!

JAN CRAWFORD, NELSON

Olga and Hank bent over their astronaut son in concern. Why this sudden post-space year depression?

"It's Julvernia — we met on Moon-Visit — but where in the galaxy is she now?"

"Yuri, son!" they both chorused. "Didn't we tell you — men are from Mars, and women from Venus!"

ELISABETH DEUCHAR, BIRKDALE

The investigating homicide detective smeared mint sauce over the succulent slices of roast leg of lamb and pondered the missing clue. What heavy blunt instrument could inflict such severe head injuries, and where was it? The newly bereaved widow defrosted her freezer and watched the unsuspecting detective eat the evidence.

J REYNOLDS, KAIAPOI

To Deal with the Devil

"**A**nd in return for your soul?"

"I want beautiful women lavishing attention on me for the rest of my life."

"So be it."

He found himself backstage at a fashion show. Suddenly he collapsed as pain filled his chest.

His last sight on Earth was of models gathering around him.

J DEPREE, CHRISTCHURCH

The Week That Was

He lay in bed stretching luxuriantly. He reflected back over his life and all that had happened to him. His had been a satisfying existence, although it had passed somewhat in a blur. It was Saturday and he wondered what lay in store for him today. Poor old Solomon Grundy.

STEVE WYN-HARRIS, WAIPUKURAU

OFFICIAL REPORT ON ALIEN MATING BEHAVIOUR

"Two gender-differentiated creatures press their digestive tract entrances together, then exchange digestive juices by entwining the muscular appendages within the upper alimentary cavities. The forelimbs engage in mutual carapace removal, using mobile palps which terminate these limbs. In this soft-bodied state, mating occurs, usually taking . . . "

"Shut up, and kiss me!"

HEATHER BELL, WHANGAPARAOA

Josie is wrapping her lips around a Big Mac hamburger.

Eileen, ever-conscious of her waistline, looks on with something approaching envy.

"Aren't you worried about your weight?" she asks.

"Oh no," Josie says, sighing with contentment, "that's what I love about fast food. There's no wait."

JOAN JARDEN, ORIENTAL BAY

INTEMPERANCE

She had had too much to drink and staggered into the room clutching another bottle, stood swaying in the doorway before falling backwards to sit on the floor, spilt drink all down her new dress.

My wife approves of all this, but personally I am against demand feeding of infants.

W M (BILL) PARSONSON, HAMILTON

A FAIRY TALE

Once upon a time a wicked sorcerer turned a handsome prince into a frog.

"Your only hope of release is to find a beautiful princess who can write your story in fifty words," he cackled.

The prince searched frantically everywhere.

Then he found me.

And we lived happily ever after.

KAY WUTZLER, PICTON

Unrequited Death

"How exciting," cooed Mrs Bainbridge, eighty-six-and-three-quarters, clutching her Last Will and Testament.

She confronted Jesus on the mantlepiece: "See?" She waved the document under His nose like a child waves her pass demandingly at the ticket-taker: "Can I go now?"

Mrs Bainbridge, eighty-six-and-three-quarters, nodded expectantly, "Please?"

Kari-Ann West, Nelson

It had been a smooth flight and Molly hurried into the terminal. Stopping, she searched the crowd for that familiar smile, feeling certain she had reminded Tom to meet the five-fifteen plane. Tom, sitting at the station, looked at his watch. The five-fifteen train must be late, he thought.

Tony Broome, Christchurch

A Deaf Ear

She suffered frequent abuse and assaults. Her hearing was permanently damaged through a strike to her head.

He now lay in bed, his breathing laboured, his chest racked with pain.

"Help me, get a doctor," he ordered.

"I can't hear you," she said, then had her first peaceful night's sleep.

BARBARA ADAMS, TAWA

Marion Goodly stepped out from her immaculate house. The perfect mother, perfect wife was on her way to her job as the perfect PA. Always smiling and immaculately presented, Marion nevertheless had her detractors and today was their day. Marion had a ladder up the back of her tights.

ISLAY MCLEOD, BROOKLYN

AGONY COLUMN

Dear Dorothy,

Can you please help? My beloved has fled the connubial bed and left me alone. What shall I do?

Tearfully,

Heartbroken Sue

Dear Heartbroken Sue,

I'm afraid I can't help in this particular marital breakup. You see, your beloved has fled straight to my marriage bed.

Blissfully,

Dorothy

JOYCE BEUMELBURG, NORTHCOTE

At last the day of reckoning arrived.

All the words had been spoken — now the verdict delivered.

The decision was against him — thumbs down.

He was rejected — dejected.

What had gone wrong? Where were his disciples and supporters?

Sadly, slowly, he put on his crimplene suit and started his Skoda.

Ron McMullen, Otahuhu

A Postcard from England

Dear Master,

You may have noticed my absence. I decided to escape the monotony and boredom of your abode. I am thoroughly enjoying the wonders of Covent Gardens and I highly recommend the grounds of Buckingham Palace for recuperation. I hope all grows well for you.

Your friendly Garden Gnome

Stephanie Read, Dunedin

She looked up from the real estate section of the *Herald* and said, "We'll have to sell."

"Sell what?" he asked, glancing at her, from behind the sports section.

"The house," she replied. "What's the point of having a sea view when you can't see the Sky Tower?"

HEATHER MCINTYRE, MURIWAI BEACH

Although not usually a believer in violence, Annabel found the knife satisfying, if a little slippery, as she removed the left testicle of the sleeping drunken rapist on her bed.

Rape Crisis would later say she was scarred for life by the attack.

Jonathan awoke screaming.

This was not home!

LEE HARRIS, DUNEDIN

DESSERT

"Do you like my Cranberry Pumpkin Chocolate Blancmange?"

"Oh yes, honey, it's lovely."

"It's my best recipe. I make it all the time."

"Mmmm."

"You look a little green. Are you OK?"

"I think I'm getting the flu."

It must be love, he thought, as he headed to the bathroom.

MELINDA SZYMANIK, MT EDEN

ARE YOU THERE?

He was suicidal. For months he had searched the world. Nothing. By some macabre fluke of fate he alone had escaped the nuclear holocaust that had annihilated mankind. He jumped from the top of the Empire State Building. Falling past the thirteenth floor, he heard the telephone start to ring.

H & M BUTCHER, PAIHIA

One year after the global festivities, he awaited the dawn of the true new millennium. A solitary celebration on this easternmost beach. Dismissing fanatical predictions of an ending world, he was full of eager anticipation as the stars faded in the clear night sky. But the sun did not rise.

CHRIS SPURRIER-DAVIES, WAINUI BEACH

BOOMERANG

When old Horace ran off with his secretary, friends rallied to commiserate with Gladys. An unconcerned Glad was wrapping a large parcel: "Pink bed-socks, nightcap, spare hearing-aid, dentures, laxatives, teddy, rubber ducky and a large bunch of flowers to agitate his hayfever.

"He'll be back," she giggled.

JEAN SMITH, GORE

DANCING CLASS

"I'm hopeless dancing with another partner," he said.

"I'm awkward and uncomfortable. I'd be useless in an affair. I wouldn't know where to begin. After all I've been married for twenty-five years, you know."

"I can fix that," she thought to herself.

"It works every time," he thought to himself.

TONY CATO, WANGANUI

PICTURE THIS

He started out painting landscapes, then small cubist interiors, eventually both free abstraction and the rigorous geometric type. Finally he produced a canvas covered by exquisite brush strokes in a solitary monochromatic white. He beamed. Critics could say what they liked, but now he truly understood the meaning of art.

MICHAEL WRIGHT, DEVONPORT

He drained his glass, sat back and continued his monologue:

"There's more sensuality in a raised eyebrow by Deneuve than a dropped everything by Madonna."

Looking across the table at his bulbous nose and flushed face, she thought that all he could expect from either star was a curled lip.

ALAN ASHWORTH, TORBAY

THE HUNGRY FRIDGE

Refrigerator always hungered. Its food in the cold quiet was repeatedly ransacked by after-schoolers. Dumped in the wasteland, it was found by hide-and-seekers. "Quick, in here," they whispered. Seeker did not find and went home. Muffled thumps on the air-sealed door, latched from outside, died unheard. Finally Refrigerator felt full.

PETER RAWNSLEY, PLIMMERTON

He laid the fuse. The whole town would blow. He'd be famous. Famous. On every front page, every paper, worldwide. His day, even if he wasn't there to see it. A minute past midnight. One last look at his watch. His day would go down in history. August 31, 1997.

LINDA BURGESS, PALMERSTON NORTH

KILLING TIME

"I don't have time to wait for you."

"It's time for dinner, where is it?"

"What time do you call this?"

"We're always late." And on and on it went.

"Not any more," she uttered, flipping the giant egg timer, his finely ground ashes slipping through the neck.

STEPHANIE FREWEN, HERNE BAY

He picked up the piece of wire and approached the car. Her thoughts raced — what was he going to do? What would they think when she didn't turn up at the usual time? He put his hand on the driver's door — it clicked! Tomorrow she really must join the AA!

JANINE CAMPBELL, CHRISTCHURCH

THE FIFTY-WORD STORY CONFERENCE

Words were assembling in the hall, trying to arrange themselves in interesting phrases.

"But for the grace of God."

"Gigantic" jostled "Spots" or was it "Tops"?

Suddenly there was a stunned silence.

"Once upon a time" stood on the stage, waving and laughing, two smiling words joined them: "The End".

SHIRLEY MACLEOD, OTAKI

"Lies, damned lies and you know it!" the Prime Minister shouted, pointing at his accuser. "I suggest you read the report again." He sat down triumphantly, pleased with his authoritative outburst. "I've told you before," Joan replied from the kitchen, "you shouldn't watch the television news. It only upsets you."

STEPHEN BLAKE, GREY LYNN

THE LIFT

The boy and his mother were in a lift with another woman and a man. The other woman slapped the man's face. The boy, overhearing his mother telling her friend about the incident, then exclaimed, "I didn't like that woman — she stood on my foot, so I pinched her bum!"

CAROLYN GREEN, ST HELIERS

Jim Carter and his secretary approached the hotel desk. He could feel his palms sweating. What would they call themselves? Mr and Mrs Smith?

The receptionist appeared. His wife Amanda.

"Amanda! What are you doing here?"

"I knew you weren't listening when I told you about my new job!"

ROBYN GOSSET, CHRISTCHURCH

The doctor broke the news — the disease would soon kill him. He could not take his dark secret to the grave. "I murdered Belinda Alverston," he said, and lost consciousness. He came around to find a policeman beside him.

"Good news, son! They made a mistake — you're going to live."

BRIAN CAMPBELL, GISBORNE

The Ultimate?

Tamara Vorishlov sat on the podium. She glanced at Mary, her lover. Approaching the lectern, she felt pain from her physically disadvantaged foot as the Washington winter sun outlined her mahogany features.

The black book was placed in her left hand, "Madame President, repeat after me. I swear by . . . "

D L Orr, Invercargill

While counting takings from her florist shop Geraldine looked into the wicked blue eyes of a balaclava'd thief. Dressed entirely in black and armed, he used that corny adage: "Your money or your life."

Forever topical and witty Geraldine replied, "Take my life. I need my money for my retirement."

G M Hamilton, Kerikeri

SEASIDE PICNIC

They picnicked by the edge of a cliff. He pushed her over after dessert. As she plummeted into the sea, he turned away laughing, only to stumble and follow her down. His last thought was one of regret that he had not had a second helping of strawberries and cream.

FREDA PEAKE, OTAKI

It was murder plain and simple. Worse still, I was the accused. Despite being told what to do should an emergency arise, in the heat of the moment I had neglected my duty. How could I possibly live knowing that I was single-handedly responsible for this death? Damn virtual pets.

STEPHEN BLAKE, GREY LYNN

A NIGHT OUT

Back inside, the two men relaxed over coffee. It had been a hard day carrying out high tech maintenance in extreme conditions.

"Shall we hit the town tonight? Go clubbing?"

"Is there any action out there?"

They looked out at the rocky surface of Mars.

"Another round of poker then?"

MARGARET BEVERLAND, ST HELIERS

ROAD RAGE

Taking her bag, Rosemary walked to the car and drove off slowly. A vehicle behind tooted loudly, then came alongside, the passenger gesticulating and yelling. It passed her, stopping to block a narrow bridge. Rosemary grasped an umbrella. The passenger approached, shouting, "Your bag will fall off the car's roof!"

JOAN MONAHAN, PONSONBY

FAMILY VALUES

When Lennie got weekend leave he found Dad doing unmentionable things with a sheep, Mum blissfully clutching a half-empty whisky bottle, Brucie happily stoned out of his skull, and Debbie performing serious body piercing with curtain rings.

Lennie's heart swelled with emotion. "Prison's cool," he thought, "but home's AWESOME."

BETTY LIVINGSTON, PALMERSTON NORTH

FEAR

First she sensed something, then she heard footsteps accelerating along the darkened street as he gained ground. Her pulse pounded and quickened as he drew level. He grasped at her sleeve, eyes darting. Not another soul in sight. A hand suddenly thrust towards her. "You dropped your purse," he said.

SANDY WINTERTON, MELROSE

Conquest

Tom returned to claim Mary.

"I told you before you left, as long as I'm alive — even after I'm dead — you'll not marry my daughter."

"We'll see about that," sneered Tom as he drew out a pistol and shot the other.

"I can't marry you," said Mary, "I'm a nun."

J S Fisher, Christchurch

Unloved

George had only himself to blame. Instead of caring more, spending more money on her, taking her out occasionally, he chose instead to neglect her. Friends called him a fool, said he'd lose her if he wasn't careful; and they were right.

When launched, she sank within minutes, almost drowning him.

Ron McIntosh, Whangarei

THE LETTER

The Registrar's letter will verify his tale: years of searching, until his brown eyes drew him to the wharenui. Late night korero revealed memories of a baby lost by adoption.

Re-christened with chanted karakia he felt belonging, wholeness. Now opening the letter he sees his father's name: Enrico Cortez, seaman.

PETER PARKER, POINT CHEVALIER

POETIC DUEL

Two poets confronted each other in a crowded hotel bar, their hip pockets bulging ominously. They drew their volumes simultaneously and fired blank verse and rhyming couplets at one another.

Mercifully there were no casualties except for a sensitive critic who was injured in a cross fire of sentimental sonnets.

JIM EDWARDS, MISSION BAY

Four am. Phone rings. I reach across the darkness. A cigar butt and whisky glass clatter. I collar the blower, growling:

"Yeah? Stinky Ratso, PI."

"Stinky, my friend, it's my wife. She's missing!"

I know that desperate voice — Clem! I look down at the blonde stirring beside me. Another case solved.

CHRISTINE STEPHENS, ASHHURST

ONE MAN'S MEAT

There was unusual activity in the house. All the servants ran hither and thither obeying the high steward's orders. In the barn the animals listened curiously to the humans' busy hum.

"What is causing this?" asked the old cow.

"I hear the young master has returned," replied the fatted calf.

PAULA BROKER, CHRISTCHURCH

Re-Creation!

Let there be light, and there was. He always loved that bit. Steadily he worked his way through the week. All was completed to his satisfaction. It was now the seventh day. The so-called day of rest. Reluctantly he trudged over to the lawn mower and pulled the cord.

STEVE WYN-HARRIS, WAIPUKURAU

Sue was depressed about work, home, telly. Randall seemed oblivious, transfixed by cathode rays.

Sue's chance net encounter with Fred brought cyber love, secret vows, new reason.

They grew old together, surfing in sync.

Flesh inconsequential, passion endured.

Randall never knew.

At night he dreamt he was abducted by aliens.

LEE HARRIS, DUNEDIN

Caught in the Act

Slowly moving backwards and forwards
Gently
Rhythmically
Caressing pink flesh
Tongue flicking, side to side
Lost in the rhythm
Moving faster and faster
Stimulating one little intimate place
And then another
Nearly there
Nearly . . .
SNAP!!!
An abrupt ceasing of movement!
The dental floss hangs limply
Caught between two hostile molars!

LYNNE ROBINSON, HAMILTON

These fifty-word stories are easy.

I just think of any subject.

"My neighbour," for instance.

At full moon, I crawl through the hedge in my Gucci underwear, clutching a magnum.

She waits in her diaphanous nightgown, standing in front of the garden lights . . .

See! Fifty words are up already!

BARRY BAIN, ARROWTOWN

I smile at his ritualistic "Spectacles, testicles, wallet and watch". He combs his hair and beard (with my comb), gives me a quick kiss, and cycles off home. I feed the cats and pour myself another drink. Will his wife, I wonder, ask him what sort of day he's had?

SALLY HUNTER, CHRISTCHURCH

CRAFTY NEIGHBOUR

"Got a permit to build that thing, mate?" he called over the fence.

"Yeah."

"Didn't come up at Council meeting."

"Went higher than that."

"To the Regional Authority?"

"No, higher."

"God Almighty!"

"That's right!"

Josh went inside and said to his wife, "He's a cocky sod, that Noah next door!"

R PHILIPS, CHRISTCHURCH

ADDICTED

Fifty. Well, forty-nine. Oops, she would have to be more disciplined, this could get out of hand. Damn, thirty-three left. Thirty. Nearly half gone.

It always turned out like this. Sated, yet greedy for more. Fifteen! So unreasonable. Why only fifty? Why couldn't they invent a three-layer chocolate box?

ROBERT SIMPSON, NAPIER

I know I put them here! Only two minutes ago. They can't just disappear . . .

Calm down, think: I put them here, then I took out the rubbish. Oh God, the truck's been. They've gone forever!

A year passes. "This compost is beautiful, our best ever. What's this, composted keys?"

JENNY WOODLEY, PLIMMERTON

Daunting challenge

Discovery, drafting.
Absorbing ideas.
Stray notions —
Fragmented facts —
Captured.
Late nights,
Bleary eyes,
Converging print.
Wastepaper basket —
Overflowing.
Myopic gaze,
Blank mind —
Writer's block!

Reflection, revision,
Ideas evolving.
Motivation, communication,
Concentration, organisation.
Purpose.
Accurate phrases,
Fluent expression.
Clear thoughts —
Writer's cramp!

Exhilaration —
Anguishing birth-pains,
A story is born!

ROSEMARY FRANCIS, LYTTELTON

H'ALLITERATIVE TALE

Harry hurried home, hoping his housekeeper had heated his hamster's herbs.

"Hello!" he hurrahed to his hirsute hamster.

However, the hamster's hutch hasp was history and Hildegard (his hamster) had hopped it.

Harry howled, horrified.

"Hildegard!" he hollered. "Hie hither, honey!"

Happily, Hildegard heeded Harry' heart-felt homily and hastened home.

ROB SCHRODER, NORTHLAND

Out of the corner of his eye he noticed her standing at the very stern of the ship and, longing for her tender embrace, he urgently wanted to kiss her; when she turned and jumped, he wondered about the colour of her eyes and whether she had smiled at him.

NORBERT SCHAFFOENER, LAINGHOLM

Two women share a train compartment — each aware of the other's overwhelming, but suppressed grief.

"I have just lost a beloved son in tragic circumstances," said one.

"How strange," said the other. "So have I."

"My son was called Jesus," said the first.

"Mine was called Judas," said the other.

WYNNE CRAILL, GISBORNE

I ran from the Carisbrook tunnel for my first All Black game.

Disaster! Ripped my shorts on the gate.

I quickly changed on the sideline. The crowd whistled.

I raced to join the waiting team.

Horrors!

In the pocket of my torn shorts were the words for the National Anthem.

BARRY BAIN, ARROWTOWN

VERSACE MODEL

She unlocked the door and stepped into the rarified atmosphere of the exclusive boutique.

Moving to a rack of dresses, she stroked the gleaming material. A Versace model caught her eye and she sighed longingly.

How lucky I am to work here, she thought, gathering up her broom and duster.

JILL WOODS, HAMILTON

THE LETTER

With hands numbed by the Northern winter, he scrawled:
"Every day, trainloads go up from this camp. You'd wonder where they went."

In the Southern winter she sat, rigid in her chair, the letter from the lieutenant in her lap . . . "He died in a soldierly way at Messines," it said.

PETER LUCAS, NELSON

When the corpse of Hone O'Malley — sheep shearer, bon vivant, and Speights drinker — floated into Mrs Dingleby Smyth's whitebaiting net she was utterly mortified when she realised that he was wearing an identical dress to the one she had recently worn to ladies' night at the last Rotary "do".

LORRAINE CRAIGHEAD, BALCLUTHA

Isolated, dark, silent, the cottage appeared in the car headlights. Alexander stopped, opening the boot to reveal Vanessa's lifeless body.

"Well," he snarled, "the bitch should have thrown me a birthday party." He was heaving her into the disused well when friends burst out of the cottage shrieking "Surprise, surp . . . !"

ANN B HOLMES, REDCLIFFS

STEPPING STONES

Benjamin tugged his boots on.

"Over, twist, pull. Loop, loop. Loop over, poke, pull."

The ties parted. Chubby fingers tried again.

Success! A whole half bow! Repeat.

Two snakes dangled.

"Aww, that'll do." A whistle sounded.

Standing, six years tall, he shambled on to the field,
laces flapping, face beaming.

LORRAINE BLAIN, NELSON

Whack! Take that, Mr Chairman and all you Board members. Further blows sent the deputy and first assistant sprawling. Strategic strikes bowled the tedious teachers and the whingeing parents. Finally, precise jabs prodded the obnoxious kids out of sight.

Game won. The school principal did enjoy his weekly pool night.

H STACE, WELLINGTON

She was contemplating the household chaos when her sister phoned to invite herself to stay.

In considerable panic, cartons of junk were hidden, windows polished, the fridge defrosted, car vacuumed and the cat de-flead. The sister arrived, wearing rubber gloves.

"I'll give you a hand to clean up," she said.

JENNY WILLIAMS, EASTBOURNE

ISLANDS

Delirious from the intensity of his attention, she dove from the isolation of her island into the ocean of desire.

She floated on his love, drifted in his indifference, floundered in his absence, drowned in her own need.

The pain of loss taught her how to swim.

CLAIRE GRIFFIN, WELLINGTON

BABY

As she lay on the bed, she could hear him rustling about. She wasn't used to this and was a little apprehensive.

Suddenly he was beside her. "I'm ready whenever you are," he said.

As he gently placed his hand on her tummy, she felt the start of another contraction.

STEPHEN SCHULZ, MT EDEN

TETE-A-TETE

They sat opposite, thirty-five years apart. He tall, pale, breakable; she vibrant, tanned, pliable and pretty. Father — daughter? Adulterer — mistress? Gold-digger? I wondered. Our eyes met. Hers flickered wide and she put her hand on top of his knee and leaned forward intimately to whisper in his ear.

TONY SVENSON, OTANE

Friday Night at the Imperial

When Buck said Tom cheated, Tom kicked Buck in the groin. Rocky broke Tom's nose, so Charlene threw a jug at Rocky. Karen scratched Charlene's eyes, Fred stabbed Rocky's chest, and Bluey smashed a glass in Mac's face. Then Buck knocked over Fred's beer — that is when things turned nasty.

GRAHAME GILLESPIE, KELBURN

The Cake

I'm in a dilemma. A prized family recipe handed down over generations and my neighbour has asked for a copy.

Finally I sit down, resign myself to the inevitable, and begin to write. She is delighted. My smile is benevolent.

After all, two missing ingredients shouldn't make that much difference.

JENNY POPE, MAIRANGI BAY

MUTUAL

Lynch let himself into the house, knowing his wife would be out. He took the note he had written saying, "I've left and won't be back" to prop it against the clock. An envelope addressed to him was already there. His wife had written, "I've left and won't be back."

A M A PHARAZYN, STORTFORD LODGE

CHECK THIS OUT

She was surrounded. She had to escape, but she couldn't leave her precious cargo. She's scoured the papers all week, she'd fought to get what she wanted. Panic gripped her — she clutched her prize as dizziness hit.

I must hold on.

"Aren't these supermarket queues dreadful?" said a voice nearby.

ROBYN WELLS, CHRISTCHURCH

The Lady of Learning

"**N**o", with appropriate gestures, was her limited communication until her third birthday.

Shy, she learnt slowly until adolescence sparked a love of words, ideas and logic.

Teaching became her fulfilment; debating, her hobby.

I visited her at the Rest Home.

"May I read to you?"

Nodding, smiling fleetingly, she murmured, "No . . . "

BETTY VALENTINE, MOSGIEL

St Peter met Johnny Do-good at the gates of Heaven. Said Johnny, adjusting his halo: "I haven't worshipped other gods nor false idols, taken the Lord's name in vain, profaned the Sabbath, dishonoured my parents, killed, adulterated, thieved, lied or coveted." Said St Peter, "You've missed one. You haven't lived."

SIMON COOKE, AVONHEAD

THE HITCHHIKER

"I'm going all the way to Wellington. Any good?"

She climbed in gratefully.

"Where have you come from?"

"Mount Eden."

She didn't want to talk, was asleep in ten minutes. He turned on the radio. " . . . has escaped from Mount Eden prison. Do not approach her, she is armed and dangerous."

LESLEY SHAW, KELBURN

SURPRISE ENCOUNTER

I planned to surprise him, but there he was, walking towards me with a woman I did not know. He touched her, bent to speak to her and they laughed at some shared pleasure.

Later, at home, I said nothing to him of what I'd seen. I was surprised at my indifference.

ROSEMARY NORMAN, EASTBOURNE

An Old Story

I did enjoy the meal and your company.

Do come up for a coffee.

No, never on a first date.

I really love you, trust me.

Oh, dear. Overdue! Worry and anxiety. Pregnant?

Marry you? My studies — I am going to be a doctor.

Abortion? No!

Your problem then.

Men!

ALWYN LANDRETH, CROMWELL

She had promised to call him when her infatuation with the bronzed lifeguard wore off. Now, weeks later, all hope had gone. How could he continuing living? This was the end, but as he stepped off the cliff edge he heard the ringing of his cellphone in his hip pocket.

DAVID LATTIMORE, LYTTELTON

Her fax from England — "Father dead. Company mine." — coalesced his plans.

A fatal reunion at Huka Falls with his hated, cowed rich wife would accomplish everything.

She arrived; elegant, svelte. "I'm successful," she said, "studying management, law and . . . "

Enraged, he pounced. The body tumbled into the Falls.

". . . Karate!" she said.

MARY ASHFORD, WAIRARAPA

SILENCE

Profound deafness had made the old man curmudgeonly. Since his beloved wife died there had been no one to interpret the rackety world for him. Sitting sleepily in the sun, he murmured, "Betty, why did you leave me?" And he clearly heard her answer, "Come too, sweetheart." So he did.

STEPHANIE TILL, HAVELOCK NORTH

THE HYPOCRITE

"The last time," she tells her family emphatically. "Absolutely, positively the last time I'm having lunch with that crowd. They are brainless and boring and smug. I'd rather eat a sandwich in the park!" The telephone rings.

She answers. "Lunch? Tomorrow? Bellamys? Of course, Jim, I'd be delighted. Thank you!"

PHILLIPA NILSON, DANNEVIRKE

"Fabulous interlude, darling! Businessmen should always take their secretaries overseas — but collect your bag and return to the office independently. Just one last kiss."

He passed through to where his wife waited. Striking him with her handbag she fumed, "A very tender moment we just saw on the overhead screen."

JOHN BARWICK, ST HELIERS

103

FIFTY WORDS

What makes you think you can write a story using only fifty words? Tandem says I can.

You're up to twenty-one. What happens next?

The following chapters consist of editors arguing over the quality of submissions.

The finale has me in the limelight receiving the Grand Prize.

So there! Satisfied?

ROBERT ALAN GILLETT, WAIHEKE ISLAND

DISQUALIFIED

Eager to overtake before the final bend, I nearly clipped the wheels on my right but was then beautifully placed for a final desperate run between slower traffic to a big flourish at the finish line. "Sorry sir," she said, "only eight items or less. This is the express checkout."

W M (BILL) PARSONSON, HAMILTON

Generation Ex

Contemplating unprotected sex with Walter, Sarah, a somewhat unethical serologist, had tested his blood. Now she tells him, "You have very little time left."

Walter gapes. "How long?"

"Who knows? Three years, three days, three minutes?"

"Is there nothing you can do?"

Sarah shrugs. "I could boil you an egg."

JOHN SMYTHE, KELBURN

Railway Junction

We sit, three feet away, each cocooned in our own direction.
I don't know you, yet I look into your soul through your eyes.
Your journey opposes mine, secretly contained in your mind.
Gently you glide away, giving me the illusion of my own start.
Then, shuddering, I go on.

NOELEEN SHAW, REMUERA

Letting Go

They are a couple no more.

At parties — it always happens now — they greet each other cautiously. Maintain their painful distance.

But cannot keep apart all night.

They'll meet for drinks, at food, or by the stereo.

Talk long in a corner.

Dance.

Hold hands.

And leave together.

HUNTLY ELIOTT, MT EDEN

He felt depressed after the long tiring drive back home, following a day exercising his keen mind on so much dishonesty. Now there was the paperwork to do, complicated questions that baffled him. It was no good, his wife would have to complete his District Court travel claim for him.

PHILIP ANDREWS, ROTORUA

Helen and Troy, both exceptionally ugly, met under unusual circumstances. She was attending the Last Chance Plastic Surgery Clinic, he was the gardener. Unable to help, the clinic had offered him a job instead.

It was true love. They got married, had exceptionally ugly triplets and lived happily ever after.

AMANDA CLOW-HEWER, ONERAHI

Six-thirty. The alarm jangled and Kate leapt out of bed in action, anxious to get everything shipshape.

Rustle, bustle, polish, dust, straighten, hide.

"Hurry up, kids, off to school."

Spring flowers in vase.

Nine o'clock. The door bell rang and Kate smiled, ready to meet the new cleaning lady.

SHONA BEGG, CHRISTCHURCH

Surprise!

When Lionel in a jealous rage pushed her off the pier, he knew she couldn't swim.

"Just retribution for her Thursday secret trysts with another man," he rationalised, walking away.

She accompanied the police when they arrested him.

"I was having swimming lessons on Thursdays to surprise you," she explained.

Zoe Battersby, Picton

A True Story

The small brothers were having a birthday party. Their mother bought for them two fine balloons. She said to James, "You are the youngest so you may choose. Do you want the red one or the blue?" James considered in silence, then said firmly, "I want the one John wants."

Susan Gatti, Kaikohe

In love, the fisherpeople decided to tie the knot.

"A simple under-n-over affair," she said, "sheepshank or butterfly."

He said, "I wants m'somethin' grand, lady . . . double-marlin hitch, a terminal knot!"

She said, "I's ain't gettin' me in no strangle-hold, mister, no constrictor-hitch!"

Later, he found the refrigerator note: "Gone fishin'."

FRITH WILLIAMS, PAEKAKARIKI

TELL JIM HICKEY IT'S NOT HIS FAULT

Six o'clock. Myrtle carefully lifts the doily. Momentarily she imagines a world without telly. She remembers Charlie Waldron who lost 189 days to rain last year. Charlie went soft after the bank foreclosed. His parting words had been, "Tell Jim Hickey it's not his fault. Wish him well from me."

JAMES DICKSON

After that cold silence of years, Prue had left.

Dairying now, in overalls and gumboots, tied to the dawn and fifty lactic cows.

She missed the city.

She laughed when she recalled dancing to John Travolta in the mirror.

Married too young, they had all said.

Married too old now.

JERRY FULFORD, BLACKBALL

BIG, MEAN AND UGLY

He appeared from nowhere; big and ugly with demon tattoos striding up his arms. Moira tried to pass but he blocked the way. He reached out to touch her baby. Moira stood still, paralysed.

He sensed her fear. "You have a beautiful baby," he said softly, before he walked away.

KATHARINE DERRICK, WHANGAREI

INDEX OF CONTRIBUTORS